TopReaders

Weather

Denise Ryan

Contents

What is the weather like?
Is it raining? Is it hot?
You can find out all about
weather in this book.

Clouds

Clouds are made of tiny drops of water. Clouds can be high up in the sky or close to the ground.

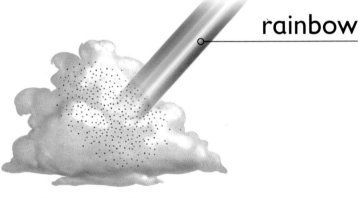

rainbow

fluffy cloud

Different kinds of clouds cause different kinds of weather.

high clouds

wispy clouds

fluffy clouds

Rain

Raindrops form when drops
of water crash together
in the clouds.

rain

Rain falls from the clouds
when the drops become too heavy.

rain clouds

Snow

Snowflakes form when
the air is freezing cold.

heavy snow

Heavy snow
has made
a tree fall down.

Floods

Floods can happen
if it rains hard
for a long time.

This is a dangerous flood.
Floods can kill people
and damage buildings.

flood

Lightning

Lightning is a giant spark
in the sky. It makes the air around
it very hot.

lightning flash

As the air gets really hot
it makes a booming sound.
That's thunder!

Tornadoes

Tornadoes are wild winds.
They can tear up trees
and destroy buildings.

tornado

Sunshine

In sandy deserts the sun shines nearly every day.

It is always hot, dry, and sunny in this sandy desert.

hot, sandy desert

Dust Storms

Dust storms happen when strong winds blow sand and dust from Earth's dry surface.

Dust storms can cover houses and farms.

dust storm

Where It All Happens

Our weather forms
in the atmosphere.

The atmosphere is a mixture
of gases above Earth.

Earth

atmosphere

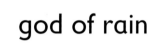

god of rain

god of thunder

Weather Myths

There are many stories about weather. Some of them are true, but some of them are not.

god of wind

goddess of lightning

god of clouds

People used to think that gods and goddesses caused the weather.

Quiz

Can you match each
weather picture with its name?

cloud   tornado

lightning   snow